gardens by design ❧ THE NATIONAL TRUST

irises

JAMES PARRY

First published in 2004 by
National Trust Enterprises Ltd
36 Queen Anne's Gate, London SW1H 9AS

www.nationaltrust.org.uk

Cataloguing in Publication Data is available from the British
Library

ISBN 0 7078 0367 5

Design and illustration by Barbara Mercer
Colour origination by Digital Imaging Ltd
Printed and bound in Hong Kong by Printing Express Ltd

Front cover: 'Kent Pride', a striking reddish-brown
and yellow bearded iris.

Back cover: Close-up overhead shot of the Siberian
iris, 'Placid Waters'.

Page 1: Dramatic close-up of an iris at Sissinghurst
Castle, Kent.

Page 2: 'Dusky Challenger' – detail of beard and
fall.

Contents

Introduction

The iris has enjoyed a close association with man for thousands of years. Its significance is such that it has transcended a role as a beautiful and useful flower, to one in which it has been perceived to represent life, love and death. That it should have achieved such iconic status tells us much about the authority and charm of a plant that continues to enthral as powerfully today as it did in antiquity.

    The Ancient Greeks had a particular fascination for the iris, its importance vested in the deity of that name. In Homer's *Iliad*, Iris was the messenger of the gods, specially dedicated to the service of Hera, the wife of Zeus, and one of the main means of communication between the heavens and the earth. She would descend on a rainbow, and was forever associated with a blaze of colour. According to some traditions, she was also the mother of Eros (who was fathered by Zephyr, the god of winds) and so inextricably linked with sensuality. Yet her responsibilities included the leading of the souls of dead women to the Elysian Fields, and it is in honour of this duty that the Greeks traditionally planted irises on the graves of women. This association with death and funereal rites was also known to the Egyptians, whose pharaohs believed that the iris would protect them in the afterlife. The flower was also an emblem of pharaonic authority and the inspiration for the sceptre, its three standard petals symbolising faith, wisdom and valour. Three has long been a significant and mystical number, and its prominence in the structure of the iris was not lost on the Christians, for whom the flower came to represent the Trinity. Such veneration was not restricted to the West, either; the iris has long carried religious significance in the Near and Far East, especially in Japan, where *Iris ensata* is the national flower and the subject of much ceremony and attention.

Sibirica iris 'Tycoon' at Sissinghurst Castle, Kent.

(Opposite): *Sibirica* iris detail.

There are some 300 species of wild iris, distributed throughout the northern hemisphere (no true irises occur naturally south of the equator) and found in a wide variety of habitats, from deserts through lowland marshes to woodlands and mountain pastures. In Britain, however, there are only two potentially native irises: *I. pseudacorus* or 'Yellow Flag', a common plant found near water throughout the British Isles, and *I. foetidissima* or 'Stinking Iris', a much more local plant found mainly in woodland and on sheltered banks, and which may in any case have been introduced here by the Romans. Meanwhile, *I. germanica* – the so-called 'German Flag' (although it is native not to Germany but to southern Europe) – is a regular garden escape and one of the most important original 'parents' of the huge number of modern-day cultivated varieties of bearded iris now available commercially.

The Iris in Art

Few plants can make as strong a claim to a place in the history of human artistic expression as the iris. From ancient frescoes to domestic wallpaper and contemporary poster art, the iris is a recurring subject and motif. It appears not only as a naturalistic expression of its true form, but also as the inspiration for the highly stylised 'fleur-de-lys', which has proved to be one of the most durable and defining decorative symbols (*see p.14*).

The oldest known representation of the iris in art is on the walls of the Minoan palace complex at Knossos on Crete. Two stucco wall decorations, dated to the middle of the second century BC, feature irises. One shows the figure of a young man walking through a meadow of stylised irises, the other is of a lapis lazuli-coloured bird among various plant

The 'Priest-King', a detail from a relief painting in the palace at Knossos.

An Iris Plant and Butterfly, from the Dara Shikuh Album, Mughal, *c*. 1635. Opaque watercolour and gold on paper. India Office Library and Records, British Library, London.

species, including a group of small irises. Contemporary Egyptians may also have depicted the iris on their buildings; iris motifs were carved into the stone walls of the Temple of Amun-Re at Karnak, for example (*see* p.18).

As far as European art is concerned, depictions of flowers, including irises, appear in the borders of medieval manuscripts and as attributes in religious paintings, but it was not until the late fifteenth century that they began to feature as art subjects in their own right. The prominence of the iris in the art of this period was undoubtedly strengthened by its association with the Virgin Mary, the blue of the iris symbolising the royal blue of the Virgin's clothing. However, the religious iconography of the iris was increasingly combined with a new artistic realism, as in Albrecht Dürer's *Madonna in the Garden* (1508), which includes a very accurate depiction of the structure and form of an iris. Yet it was the passion of the increasingly secular Dutch for flowers as objects of beauty in their own right that helped drive the sixteenth- and seventeenth-century vogue in the Low Countries for autonomous flower pictures, the now celebrated 'still lifes'. Artists such as Jan Brueghel (1568–1625), Roelandt Savery (1576–1637) and Balthasar van der Ast (*c*.1594–1657) all featured irises prominently in their works. This was an age of great interest in plants and much related economic activity, as evidenced by the huge prices commanded by certain types of rare tulip bulb during the 1630s, and, to a lesser degree, by hyacinths a century or so later. Irises never wielded such commercial clout, but nonetheless they constituted a regular and popular subject for artists, especially those serving patrons with a specific interest in natural history, such as Daniel Rabel (1578–1637). Rabel worked for King Louis XIV of France and depicted such exotics as the deep-purple *I. susiana* (or 'Mourning Iris'), a species unknown in the wild and allegedly sent to Europe from Turkey by the Austrian ambassador to the Ottoman court after he found it in a Constantinople garden.

As contact between West and East grew, so the potential list of irises to illustrate grew ever longer. The Near East was a particularly rich source of material, and by the fifteenth century already had a well-developed floral art form of its own. The strictures of Islam prohibited the depiction of humans and animals, and perhaps because of this, the illustration of plants reached refined levels of sophistication and ubiquity within the sphere of Islamic art and architecture. The sensual and intricate lines of the iris made it an ideal subject for incorporation into the arts of Persia and Mughal India, for example. Although the artistic application of floral motifs in India pre-dates the ascendancy of the Mughals during the first half of the sixteenth century, the great flourishing of the arts that took place under the Emperors Jehangir and Shah Jehan (ruled 1605–1627 and 1627–1658 respectively) took the use of floral images to new heights of refinement and elegance. The 'floral style' became one of the dominant artistic and decorative expressions of the Mughal era, and one in which the iris played a significant role. Along with images of roses and tulips, depictions of irises were featured extensively in paintings, decorated books and manuscripts, were carved into marble, stone, ivory and glass, woven into carpets and assembled in pietra dura. Irises were very much plants of the Mughal heartland of Central Asia, and the dynasty's spread southwards into India, many regions of which are generally unsuitable for iris cultivation, may help explain why the iris commanded special affection for the Mughals: it reminded them of home. Their love for the iris is commemorated by an old

Detail of an iris, painted on the skirt of Queen Elizabeth I. The portrait in which this appears was commissioned by Elizabeth, Countess of Shrewsbury ('Bess of Hardwick'), who adopted the iris as one of her own motifs.

variety carrying the name of one of their illustrious emperors (see p.76).

Meanwhile, in Europe floral motifs were also moving off the canvas and onto other media, especially textiles. Flowers had always been popular subjects in embroidery and weaving, and irises appear regularly on English textiles of the Tudor period. Significantly, they were considered appropriate decorative emblems for those of the highest rank; one of their most notable appearances is on an extravagant dress worn by Queen Elizabeth I and shown in a contemporary portrait (probably of the 1580s) on display at the National Trust's Hardwick Hall in Derbyshire. The use of floral motifs served to emphasise the eternal spring of the Elizabethan era, and the choice of the iris was ideal, as it both alluded to the sensuality of the Queen while underlining her enduring virginity, through its traditional links with the Virgin Mary. By this time the impact of the iris was also becoming more apparent through the increasing use of the fleur-de-lys (see p.14).

Irises continued to feature in European art during the following three centuries, usually through the medium of still lifes or scientific botanical illustration, but it was during the nineteenth century that attention returned to the iris as a flower of emotion and power, through the works of Impressionists such as Paul Cézanne (1839–1906), Auguste Renoir (1841–1919) and, most famously, Claude Monet (1840–1926), who prolifically painted the irises in his garden at Giverny. Vincent Van Gogh (1853–90) also helped take the iris to new levels of expression and impact in art. Shortly after committing himself to an asylum at Saint-Rémy in the south of France, Van Gogh painted a series of pictures of irises, which he had found growing plentifully in the walled garden of the asylum. Their vibrant and varied colours captivated both Van Gogh and, later, art lovers and collectors worldwide; one of his iris series, *Irises* (1889), was sold in 1987 for US$54 million, at the time a record price for a painting.

During the twentieth century the iris continued to occupy an important role in art, most notably in the works of Georgia O'Keeffe (1887–1986), Cedric Morris (1889–1982) and Elizabeth Blackadder (b. 1931). Morris in particular was fascinated by irises, and in addition to his work as an artist he was highly regarded as a plantsman. His garden at Benton End in Suffolk held a spectacular collection of irises, many of which he had bred himself (see p.26).

The fleur-de-lys

Legend claims that it was King Clovis of the Franks (c.AD465–511) who first adopted the iris as a royal emblem, although the circumstances surrounding this action are unclear. One tale recounts how Clovis was presented with an iris by an angel in honour of his conversion to Christianity, whereas other stories describe how, whilst leading his forces in a campaign against the Goths, he arrived at the banks of a seemingly impassable river; he was only able to cross by riding his horse through shallow water, guided by a 'carpet of yellow flowers', quite possibly *I. pseudacorus*. In gratitude he emblazoned the iris on his banner, thereby replacing the three toads that had featured there previously! Some six centuries later, King Louis VII of France adopted the purple iris as a symbol of the royal house, allegedly following a dream he experienced shortly before leaving on a crusade to the Holy Land in 1147. The crusade was disastrous, but the three-petalled iris motif remained on the royal insignia and became known as the 'fleur de Louis'. This evolved into 'fleur de Luce' and thence to 'fleur de Lys'. The fact that 'lys' is the French for lily only served to reinforce the traditional confusion between the two plants, but there can be no doubt that it was an iris that provided Louis VII's initial inspiration. He started a tradition that continued until the abolition of the French monarchy in 1789. Indeed, so potent was the royal association with the fleur-de-lys that during the French Revolution fleur-de-lys symbols on buildings were either defaced or removed by revolutionaries, and draperies and embroideries featuring the pattern were destroyed.

Yellow Flag iris, possibly the original inspiration for the fleur-de-lys design.

Political connotations notwithstanding, the fleur-de-lys has remained a powerful heraldic device and has also become a ubiquitous artistic and decorative motif. It was used with particular enthusiasm by proponents of the Arts and Crafts movement, such as William Morris and his pupil and colleague, J. H. Dearle. Fleur-de-lys designs were especially popular on wallpaper, and Morris was also not slow to understand the appeal of a more naturalistic depiction of the iris; as early as the 1880s his company was offering several wallpaper designs featuring irises of various colours.

Four variations of the basic fleur-de-lys profile.

Uses of the Iris

The iris has been valued for its culinary, cosmetic and medicinal properties for thousands of years. Despite its potentially toxic qualities – it can act as a powerful purgative – it has been used throughout history to add flavour and aroma to food and beverages. The Ancient Egyptians made a spice from the iris rhizomes, which were used by the Greeks and Romans to enhance the taste of wine. Indeed, this practice extended to other parts of Europe; in France, for example, iris was added to certain wines and liqueurs to create a distinctive bouquet and taste, and it is still used today in Italy in the making of Chianti wine. In Germany iris was part of the beer production process, whilst in England it was added to both imported brandy and gin as a flavouring. Ground iris root was also used as a coffee substitute. In North Africa, meanwhile, iris bulbs (usually those of *Iris juncea*) were traditionally eaten as 'takouk'.

Iris products were also employed in a range of cosmetic uses. Rhizomes were chewed to help combat bad breath, and the external application of iris root juice was claimed to assist with the removal of blemishes and freckles. The Greeks extracted a fragrant oil from *I. odoratissima*, enjoyed for its cleansing properties. However, the most significant iris product was orris root, the name given to the dried rhizomes of bearded irises, primarily *I. germanica*, *I. pallida* and 'Florentina'. When dried, the rhizomes produce a fragrant odour not unlike that of violets. Orris – a derivation of 'iris' – was known to both the Ancient Greeks and the Egyptians, and put to a range of uses, from the flavouring of beverages and sweets to perfume production. It was especially valued as a fixative, serving to strengthen the scent and flavours of other substances. In certain regions of Italy, notably Tuscany, the collection of orris root was a significant local industry and 'Florentina' is named after Florence, where the commercial cultivation of orris was well established by the Middle Ages and on which city's coat of arms the iris – in the form of the fleur-de-lys – still features (see p.44). In addition to its use in perfume-making and flavouring, orris was also used commonly as a household herb, especially to give a refreshing aroma to bed linen and clothing. In the late sixteenth century, English herbalist Henry Lyte reported that 'the Iris is knowen of the clothworkers and drapers, for with these rootes they use to trimme their clothes to make them sweete and pleasant'. In medieval times, iris flowers and leaves were often strewn over household floors to reduce unsavoury domestic odours and help create an illusion, at least, of cleanliness. Furthermore, the use of iris in daily apparel was not restricted to maidens sporting flowers in their hair; orris root powder was regularly used to perfume wigs, and there are even records of dried iris rhizomes being incorporated into jewellery and rosary beads.

However, it was for its use in medicine that the iris was most widely known. Its particular properties have been appreciated for at least several thousand years and, indeed, the iris makes some of its earliest appearances in the gardens of apothecaries and herbalists. The Greek physician Dioscorides included two types of iris – *I. germanica* and 'Florentina' – in a group labelled 'the Aromatics' in his herbal, *De Materia Medica*, of the first century AD, advising that 'All of them have a warming, extenuating facultie, fitting up against coughs, and extenuating grosse humours hard to get up. They purge thick humours and choler … and heale the toments of ye belly.' The powerful cathartic and emetic effect of the plant was valued in the treatment of a wide range of ailments, from bronchitis to snake-bite and syphilis, but it was considered particularly efficacious against pulmonary complaints and coughs. In most cases the remedy was to drink the powders ground from the dried rhizomes with water or wine, and in Britain both *I. pseudacorus* and *I. foetidissima* were used medicinally in this way.

Another common medicinal use of the iris was as a remedy for dropsy, for which fresh roots were bruised in wine and the resulting juice then drunk. Accidental overdoses could be serious affairs, prompting violent bouts of vomiting and colic. Indeed, care was always necessary with the application of iris-based medicine. The celebrated English herbalist John Gerard made the following suggestion in his *Herball* of 1597: 'The root of the common Floure de-luce cleane washed, and stamped with a few drops of rose-water, and laid plaisterwise upon the face of a man or woman, doth in two daies at the most take away the blacknesse or blewnesse of any stroke or bruse.' He goes on to warn, however, that those with particularly sensitive skin would be well advised to place a piece of silk between their body and the root strips, the power of the latter being so great as to cause inflammation. Not surprisingly, the advent of modern medicine and the development of synthetic products has greatly stemmed the demand for natural iris products in recent decades. Yet the power of the iris to inflame – spiritually, emotionally and physically – remains strong.

The dramatic seeds of *Iris foetidissima* provide welcome colour in autumn.

Irises in the Garden

The history of the iris as a garden plant may date back more than 3,000 years. During the reign of the Egyptian pharaoh Thutmosis III (1540–1450BC) a series of successful military campaigns brought areas of the Levant under Egyptian control. In celebration, Thutmosis is claimed to have ordered the creation of a garden, to be stocked with plants brought back from the newly conquered lands. This 'botanical garden' is depicted in reliefs on the walls of the temple of Amun-Re at Karnak and includes representations of irises. However, it is not certain that the real garden ever existed, the relief perhaps serving more as a visual account of the landscapes encountered by the Egyptian forces in what are today Palestine and Syria. Equally, the gardens of the Ancient Greeks remain something of an unknown quantity, archaeological evidence suggesting that domestic gardens were not at all common in Greek towns and cities. However, it is possible that irises featured in courtyards as potplants. The Romans, by contrast, greatly valued domestic gardens and were certainly familiar with the iris as a garden plant. Virgil, writing in the first century BC, describes the irises in his own garden, remarking on their range of colours and on how apt it was that they carried the name of the goddess of the rainbow.

The medicinal and cosmetic uses of the iris help explain why it was regularly found in early monastic gardens and in those cultivated by herbalists. However, its decorative qualities were such that, as garden design and content became more sophisticated, so the iris became more widely planted. The *Capitulare de Villis*, a comprehensive property survey commanded by the Holy Roman Emperor Charlemagne *c.* AD800, contains references to irises in gardens, and by the first half of the fourteenth century there is evidence of their presence in Italian gardens, planted in beds alongside lilies and roses and depicted in contemporary paintings. Clearly, the iris was being taken seriously as a garden plant by this period; for example, the inventory of the garden of the Hôtel de Saint-Pol near Paris refers to the planting there in 1398 of 300 individual flag irises. Nearly three hundred years later, irises were used extensively in the planting of the royal gardens of the Tuileries, redesigned by Le Nôtre and still containing irises today.

I. germanica was perhaps the most common iris species to be found in European gardens of the fourteenth and fifteenth centuries, together with the very old cultivar 'Florentina' and *I. pallida* (see pp.44 and 48). Until the sixteenth century virtually all the iris species found in European gardens were indigenous European types of bearded iris, or at least derivations of these. For example, the genetic status of *I. germanica* was already confused by then, with the many different type variations indicating that it had been widely cultivated and hybridised for some time (it may, indeed, be a very old natural hybrid). However, interest in the more unusual varieties had always been strong – for example, the Leiden Botanical Garden maintained a collection of Spanish irises under the care of Carolus Clusius (1526–1609), and the late sixteenth-century herbalist Gerard grew at least sixteen different types of iris in his garden, including the 'great flouer de luce of Dalmatia', better known today as *I. pallida*. The plant-growers of the Low Countries played an important role in the development and introduction of early strains of iris, and during the 1600s dramatic new species were introduced to European gardens for the first time, including the first *sibirica* irises. Particularly exciting varieties of iris were brought from their native habitat in the Near East by merchants and travelling botanical scholars, which helped open the eyes of iris enthusiasts in the West to the elaborate and exotic gardens of Islam.

Innominata hybrid irises at the National Trust's Knightshayes Court in Devon.

Introduction

As early as the 1620s European irises were carried across to the New World, for planting in the gardens of newly formed colonies such as Virginia. This was the beginning of a tradition that was to see American iris-breeders play a critical role in the development of many modern iris cultivars. Meanwhile, the use of irises in gardens was changing. Traditionally, they had been planted on their own in rows or clumps in generally formal beds, often as 'set-pieces', but during the second half of the nineteenth century irises began to play their part in the ascendancy of the herbaceous border, in which they were mixed informally with other plants. In some ways this is surprising, as irises make good feature plants, but they were equally favoured by those encouraging a more naturalistic approach to garden design than the formal carpet bedding that had characterised the earlier decades of the Victorian period in Britain. William Robinson's *The English Flower Garden* (1883) and Gertrude Jekyll's *Colour in the Flower Garden* (1908) both promoted the idea of 'accepting nature as a guide' (Robinson's words), in which planting followed a palette of colour, form and texture to mirror that found in nature – even if, in reality, it was highly contrived in the garden context. Jekyll in particular was fond of the iris and incorporated it enthusiastically into her planting schemes (*see opposite*).

At the same time, the variety of irises available to gardeners was increasing rapidly. This was due partly to the discoveries of European plant-hunters travelling overseas and bringing back hitherto unknown varieties from remote China and Japan, but mainly to the work of iris breeders, who by the late nineteenth

Iris variegata or 'Hungarian Iris' is a native of central Europe.

Irises at Barrington Court in Somerset, where Gertrude Jekyll designed a stunning rose and iris garden (see p.70).

century were busy crossing various species and existing cultivars (many of which were naturally occurring hybrids) to create an impressive range of new forms and colours. This was particularly so with the bearded irises, almost all varieties of which can trace their genetic history back to *I. germanica*, *I. pallida* or *I. variegata*. The latter species, for example (*see opposite*), is the original source for almost all yellow-flowered bearded irises. French growers were instrumental in the early development of varieties of bearded iris, most notably de Bure, who in the 1820s was the first to name a cultivar and distribute it commercially. Two decades later, another French nurseryman, Lémon, published a list of over 100 named varieties of iris, but all of these were 'accidental', in the sense that they were produced naturally by bee pollination; so-called 'hand-crossing' only became widespread in the 1890s and spawned a whole new range of cultivars. Meanwhile, the nursery of Ferdinand Cayeux south of Paris became an important source of new irises (*see* pp.28 and 84).

Two key figures in British iris circles during this period were Sir Michael Foster (1836–1907) and William Rickatson Dykes (1877–1925). Foster identified and named many wild species of iris, especially those from Asia Minor, and Dykes was the leading iris authority of his time, classifying the whole family of irises in his definitive work *The Genus Iris* (1913). In his honour the iris societies of Britain, Australia and the United States (and

The tall bearded iris 'Whitehall', a beautiful cultivar but now very rare.

of France also, for a period in the 1920s and '30s) have named their top award 'the Dykes Medal'. American breeders attained prominence in the early decades of the twentieth century, among them the Sass brothers, based in Nebraska, and Bertrand Farr, who bred the celebrated 'Quaker Lady' (*see* p.68).

In 1900 most bearded irises were purple, white or yellow, or a mixture of these colours. As hybridising techniques became better understood and more sophisticated, so it became possible to develop a greater range of colours and forms. In addition, there was a growing desire to produce flowers that were more free-flowering, bloomed for longer and had a more robust structure, thereby being capable of withstanding wind, rain and disease better than some of the more traditional cultivars. In recent years this has resulted in bigger flowers, often with thicker, ruffled petals – which help give strength – and much more extravagant colour combinations. Certain breeders have concentrated on developing and refining additional features, such as 'spoons' and 'horns' (*see* 'Thornbird', p.82), resulting in the so-called 'space-age' varieties. Very recent innovations include the development of cultivars with random striping across the petals and of 'luminata' patterns, whereby the veins of a pale base colour show through an overlying dark tint.

However bold and dramatic these new irises may be, the older varieties possess both charm and historic value. In some respects they offer a more coherent and flexible colour palette for integration with other plants in the wider garden. In recent years interest in old irises has revived, particularly in the United States, and in 1988 led to the creation of the Historic Iris Preservation Society, dedicated to the promotion of traditional varieties and to the identification and sourcing of 'lost' cultivars.

Iris Characteristics

All irises have the same upright shape, with the flowers appearing either along, or at the end of, a spike or spikes. Iris flowers have six petals in total, three inner and three outer. In many species the former stand upright at the centre of the flower and are known as standards; the outer petals – called falls – are often larger than the standards, flaring out and downwards. The beard that gives bearded irises their name runs vertically along the middle of each fall (*see* diagram, p.24) and serves to direct insects towards the flower's pollen. Irises vary hugely in terms of height; some of the tall bearded cultivars can grow not far short of two metres high, whereas the more diminutive *Reticulata* and *Juno* varieties may only reach a few centimetres or so.

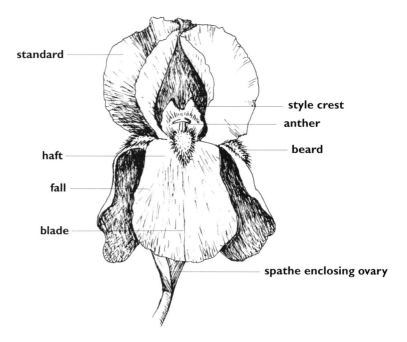

standard

style crest

anther

beard

haft

fall

blade

spathe enclosing ovary

Iris leaves are mostly long, thin, pointed and deciduous, dying back totally in winter. Most varieties of iris favour well-drained soil and full sun, are reasonably hardy and flower from spring to early summer, although some varieties will bloom twice within a season – so-called 'remontants'. Bearded irises usually carry several flowerheads along the spike, each one opening in sequence and generally not lasting more than two days. Most irises enjoy being 'baked' by the sun during their dormant mid- to late summer period, the obvious exception being the so-called water irises, many of which do, however, prefer damp (rather than completely wet) conditions.

Iris taxonomy is a complex subject. Broadly speaking, irises can be divided into two main groups, rhizomatous and bulbous, and there are a large number of sub-groups within this arrangement. Bearded irises, with which this book is mostly concerned, form one of three sub-groups within the rhizomatous group, the others being beardless irises (which includes the Pacific Coast, *sibirica* and *spuria* varieties, as well as the *laevigatae* or water irises, including the 'Japanese Iris', *I. ensata*) and crested irises. Bearded irises are sub-divided according to height – dwarf, intermediate and tall – which is also the sequence in which they tend to flower, the dwarf being earliest. The bulbous group of irises include the *reticulatas*, celebrated for their early flowering season – they appear in January in milder areas – and the *junos*, also at their peak in early spring.

Two popular misconceptions about irises are that they all flower for a couple of weeks only in spring to early summer, and that their flowers are predominately blue or yellow. Neither is true. Certainly, individual irises are only in bloom for a few days and the majority of bearded irises, for example, are at their best in early June, but careful selection of different species and cultivars will help ensure that a garden can boast a display of irises in flower continuously from January through to August or even September. Meanwhile, the range of colours now available is vast, from deep purple to crystal white, with myriad variations between. Only a genuine black or true scarlet red continue to evade iris breeders.

'Shannopin' irises at Sissinghurst Castle, Kent (*see also* p.78).

type: **tall bearded**
date: **1956**
grower: **Morris**
height: **90cm (36in)**
colour: **violet & mauve**
in flower: **mid-season**

Benton Nigel

Cedric Morris is celebrated for his strong and direct paintings of people, landscapes and wildlife. They equated to a similarly honest style in Morris's other great love, his garden. Indeed, he always referred to himself as an 'artist-plantsman' and his garden at Benton End, in Hadleigh, Suffolk, was appreciated as much by the artists and art students who came to paint there (including such luminaries as Lucian Freud) as by the plant enthusiasts who visited in their droves. Morris had moved to Benton End with his partner and fellow artist Lett Haines in 1940, and lived, worked and gardened there until his death over four decades later. He enjoyed bold plants and took great delight in filling his garden with rare and exotic species; at one time some 700 different varieties were growing there. These included a notable collection of irises, and Morris became renowned for his dedication to their care and propagation. Haines, meanwhile, showed dwindling interest in the garden. Writer Christopher Neve observed: 'Morris would get up at 6am to weed his iris beds and Haines got up and had a cocktail in a darkened room at noon.'

The iris varieties bred by Morris were given the prefix 'Benton' after their birthplace. 'Benton Nigel' was named after Nigel Scott, a young botanist who became very close to Morris. It can be found today in the Kent garden created by Vita Sackville-West and her husband, Harold Nicolson, at Sissinghurst Castle, now in the care of the National Trust. It may well have been a present to Vita, who visited Benton End to advise on old roses. Typical of the handsome and robust irises that so delighted Morris, the soft and delicate colours of 'Benton Nigel' belie a lively and bold character, so apparent in the crisp violet standards and generously proportioned falls, suffused with a range of beguiling pinks and mauves and overset by a delicate purple beard.

Sadly, Morris's wonderful garden did not survive many months beyond his death in 1982. Benton End was sold, and with the garden falling into disrepair, a group of friends and fellow iris enthusiasts dug out most of the plants and took them to new, welcoming homes. Some found their way to the garden of Beth Chatto, a friend and great admirer: 'Gardens often don't last, but the ideas and knowledge can be passed on. The essence of Cedric's ideas … have spread like yeast throughout the country. I learned from him that plants we have care of are not our plants, they should be for everyone' (*Gardens Illustrated*, February 2003).

type: **tall bearded**
date: **1932**
grower: **Cayeux**
height: **90cm (36in)**
colour: **blue/grey & lavender**
in flower: **mid-season**

Béotie

This is a rather strange and beguiling iris. Its subtle and unusual colours are not immediately to everyone's taste and yet once appreciated, it exerts a great fascination. 'A very lovely iris, but one which will only appeal to the few with a discerning eye', claimed the irrepressible iris experts Major and Mrs Murrell (see p.90), after examining it in France. The delicately veined tissue-paper quality of the pale standards, a sort of elephant-grey suffused with pink, can give it an almost ghostly appearance, as if it were floating in mid-air. The falls are a rich lavender, also spun with blue and of strong yet elegant form. Indeed, the overall shape of the flower is quite outstanding, and among the most voluptuous of any iris. However, 'Béotie' failed to win the French Dykes Medal, beaten on the day by the dramatic yellow self, 'Éclador'. It is now a rather elusive cultivar, and a precious find anywhere.

One lucky owner is Jim Marshall, for many years a gardens adviser to the National Trust, who harbours one in his garden in Suffolk: 'The combination of flower colour is breathtaking, even if it is not the most prolific in flower production. It reminds me of a summer sky just before a thunderstorm, and is just as electrifying.'

'Béotie' was grown by Ferdinand Cayeux, whose nursery at Petit-Vitry near Paris became the foremost French source of irises, especially new cultivars, and a place of pilgrimage to all those interested in irises and their development during the 1920s and '30s. Cayeux was a prolific hybridiser, dominating French iris production, and his reputation was second to none: 'Having spoken to iris specialists and amateurs alike, whom I have met in England and in France, I believe the general opinion to be that Monsieur Cayeux is currently the most advanced hybridiser in the world. This opinion is as strong in England as it is in France,' claimed one American visitor to his nursery. Cayeux regularly imported irises from England and America, using them to develop new cultivars of his own, and he was famed for his concentration on the aesthetic appearance of his hybrids: in true French fashion, he bred for style. The nursery he founded continues to flourish today (see 'Provençal', p.66, and 'Vive la France', p.86).

type: **tall bearded**
date: **1975**
grower: **Hamblen**
height: **85cm (34in)**
colour: **yellow & mauve**
in flower: **early / mid-season**

Betty Simon

This is an iris with undeniable glamour, a quality expressed perfectly by plantsman Michael Loftus of Woottens nursery in Suffolk: 'A favourite iris for me. I like to pick a great bunch of it to put in front of a silver Venetian mirror.' Exactly so. Indeed, it is hard to imagine 'Betty Simon' looking anything less than ravishing, even in the most unpromising of locations. Fresh and pert in demeanour, with bright yet delicate yellow standards and matching beards over sensual violet-blue falls, she provides a soothing and peaceful presence. Planted *en masse*, the effect can be magnificent and it is a shame that one does not often see irises such as this planted in drifts, the great 'iris canals' advocated by Gertrude Jekyll.

The individual shape of the flowerhead is also interesting, insofar as it is decidedly less regular than most modern tall beardeds; the falls have a rather open aspect and irregularly indented fringes. The overall effect is faintly reminiscent of certain types of peony, and in the views of some irisarians gives this variety the edge over the more uniformly shaped cultivars.

As if her beauty were not enough, there are other reasons for creating a space for 'Betty Simon' in the garden. The scent is strong and refreshing, reminiscent of citrus fruits and, some claim, of lemon balm. A lengthy flowering season – and many branching stems – means that in some years it is possible to enjoy an abundance of flowerheads in bloom from the third week of May to the second week of June.

A US Dykes Medal winner in 1993, the popular bicolour 'Edith Wolford' (Schreiner, 1986) is broadly similar to 'Betty Simon', but with a more robust and ruffled structure and decidedly stronger tones of yellow and violet. It is equally vigorous and freely flowering, yet for integration in a mixed border the more subtle and flexible blends of 'Betty Simon' perhaps work best. Both varieties excel, however, as feature plants in their own space.

type: **tall bearded**
date: **1934**
grower: **J. Sass**
height: **90cm (36in)**
colour: **mauve & purple**
in flower: **mid-season**

The Black Douglas

The Sass brothers – Jacob and Hans – were pioneer iris breeders in the American Mid-West, where they farmed on the open prairie near Omaha in Nebraska. They had arrived in America in 1884 as small boys with their parents from Germany, and came to combine agriculture with a deep love of botany. They first became interested in the flower species of their immediate prairie environment, which included the native *I. versicolor*, but soon established an outstanding collection of plants in their garden. Jacob, known to all as 'Mr Jake', became particularly interested in irises, and bloomed his first seedling in 1907. This was the beginning of an illustrious horticultural career that was to see both the Sass brothers introduce scores of new iris cultivars to the market over the ensuing four decades, winning many awards in the process.

Conditions in rural Nebraska were hardly straightforward for iris cultivation. In one year mice consumed 70 per cent of the brothers' seed stock, and the winters were invariably bitter and full of snow. Temperatures as low as −35°C (−30°F) induced the Sass brothers to make extensive use of the hardy species iris *I. variegata* and its derivatives in their hybridising. They did much work with yellow varieties, but also saved the dark segregates from their blue lines to try to produce a really dark cultivar. The results were patchy, with many promising new varieties reverting after the first flowering, but persistence and patience finally produced 'The Black Douglas', which at the time of its introduction was one of the darkest varieties yet seen.

'Black' is something of a misnomer, as this is really a mid- to dark-purple variety, albeit one of great beauty. The standards are a rich medium mauve, the falls of deep velvet purple overlain by a prominent beard of mauve tipped with bright yellow. The plant is most statuesque, tall and strong (as one would expect from a cultivar bred to withstand the fierce prairie winds) and with a particularly well-balanced flowerhead, the falls arching down elegantly below sculpted standards. A superb variety for the mixed border.

type: **tall bearded**
date: **1977**
grower: **Gibson**
height: **95cm (38in)**
colour: **blue & white**
in flower: **early/mid-season**

Blue Staccato

The shape and colour of 'Blue Staccato' never fails to catch the eye. This is a classic example of a plicata, the term given to irises that have a light background (usually white or yellow) with darker patterns or stippling – sometimes known as stitching – around the edges of both the standards and falls. The extent of this patterning varies greatly from one cultivar to the next, but it can create intricate, almost kaleidoscopic effects of great impact and appeal.

Whilst typical of a plicata, 'Blue Staccato' is also one of the most handsome. The plant is tall and stately, and the flared and slightly ruffled petals are beautifully presented in a combination of blue and white, the former shot with indigo; the standards have a heavy blue edging that delicately but relentlessly infiltrates the base white with thin veins, like ink on wet blotting paper. The white is very lightly flecked with blue dots, either side of the strong central vein. On the falls the edging is much more restrained, more truly marginal, and leaves an open, almost milky central shield, again with light blue speckling but also with a discernible yellow trail running from the haft vertically down the blade of each petal. The beard, yellow at its base, becomes white and then blue towards the exposed tip.

'Blue Staccato' belongs to the 'middle' generation of plicatas and represents the transition between older cultivars, such as 'Madame Chéreau' (p.62) or the delightful 'Rosy Veil' (Sass, 1953, *left*), and a new generation of more robust and extravagantly structured varieties. These include the stunning 1994 British Dykes Medal winner, 'Orinoco Flow' (Bartlett, 1989). The ability of 'Blue Staccato' to withstand the challenge of such newcomers rests not just on its beauty, however; it also has one of the strongest scents of any iris. It pours forth vanilla, in an outrageous and exotic gesture that few other cultivars can rival.

type: **tall bearded**
date: **1952**
grower: **Randall**
height: **85cm (33in)**
colour: **lavender & purple**
in flower: **mid-/late season**

Braithwaite

A handsome variety possessing both excellent shape and colour combination, 'Braithwaite' is a good example of a neglecta, the name given to those varieties of iris with pale blue standards and darker blue falls. A cross between 'Lothario' (see p.60) and the decidedly glamorous 'Helen Collingwood' (Smith, 1949), it has light lavender blue standards, sometimes so pale as to appear almost white, contrasting with dark purple falls, which are stained with indigo and pale towards the edges to produce a bleached ink effect. The beard is bright yellow.

'Braithwaite' was grown by Harry Randall, who spent most of his professional life in the electrical supply industry and was the first chairman of the London Electricity Board. When not busy managing the supply of power to the capital, he was a keen plantsman, his passion for flowers extending from roses to daffodils and hemerocallis (day-lilies). Irises were, however, his main area of interest, and he used to award collections of rhizomes to the lucky winners of the LEB staff annual flower show. President of the British Iris Society for several years, Randall was well regarded among his fellow irisarians for a no-nonsense approach to the subject. Despite the utmost horticultural credentials – he was a highly respected hybridiser and knew all of the iris 'greats' of his time, including the formidable W. R. Dykes – he was a modest man with a healthy sense of humour. He once wrote, '...for many years in business life I had to attend innumerable meetings, often listening to speeches of depressing dullness. After a while I developed the ability to allow one half of my mind to wait for the occasional word of wisdom whilst the other half thought of my irises, and I had what Wordsworth described as "a vision of that inward eye which is the bliss of solitude".'

Randall's 'Braithwaite' is still a popular variety, with a reputation as a solid performer, and it continues to make regular appearances in show gardens at Chelsea and elsewhere. The book written by its creator, *Irises*, published posthumously in 1969, remains one of the most entertaining reads on the subject.

type: **intermediate bearded**
date: **1959**
grower: **Van Veen**
height: **60cm (24in)**
colour: **pink**
in flower: **mid-season**

Constant Wattez

A true pink 'self' – an iris in which the entire flower is of one colour – was an elusive goal for early iris growers. As a recessive gene, pink tended to be dominated by other colours, especially blue (creating purple tones), and parent types with promising pink characteristics regularly failed to produce pink offspring. By the mid-twentieth century, breeders finally succeeded in breeding varieties free of other colours, and in particular away from the purple shades towards apricot and orange. 'Constant Wattez' represents a major milestone in this so-called 'pink revolution', and is still featured in plant catalogues today.

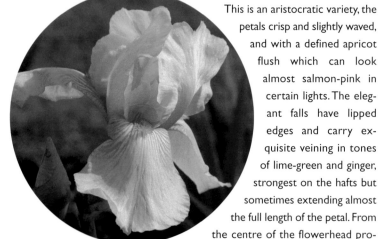

This is an aristocratic variety, the petals crisp and slightly waved, and with a defined apricot flush which can look almost salmon-pink in certain lights. The elegant falls have lipped edges and carry exquisite veining in tones of lime-green and ginger, strongest on the hafts but sometimes extending almost the full length of the petal. From the centre of the flowerhead protrudes a vibrant tangerine beard. To date, pink irises have always had orange or orange-pink beards, but with recent advances in hybridising it can only be a matter of time before new combinations are achieved.

As with all intermediate or median irises, 'Constant Wattez' is a result of the crossing of dwarf varieties with tall cultivars. This produces plants of between 41 and 70cm (16–27in) in height and which flower mid-season, ie between the dwarfs and talls. British grower William Caparne played a key role in the development of the intermediate form, and at his nursery on Guernsey he forced tall bearded varieties under glass so that their flowering period coincided with that for dwarf irises, thereby enabling him to cross them effectively.

Despite her popularity among iris-lovers, 'Constant Wattez' is not found easily in British gardens today. My only encounter with her away from the specialist nurseries was on a bright mid-June evening in a Gloucestershire garden, three plants in full bloom against a backdrop of vibrant green ferns growing on a dry stone wall. They looked delightful, and made the point that this is very much a showpiece plant, and not one to lose in a border.

type: **tall bearded**
date: **1986**
grower: **Schreiner**
height: **95cm (38in)**
colour: **deep purple**
in flower: **late season**

Dusky Challenger

The frozen wastes of Minnesota in winter seem an unpromising location in which to set up an iris nursery, but that is precisely what Francis Xavier Schreiner did in the 1920s in the town of St Paul, on the banks of the Mississippi. During the First World War Schreiner had developed an amateur interest in irises and by 1922 he had built up a sizeable collection, issuing his first catalogue two years later. This was an important period for American irisarians, with growing public interest in irises and many new varieties coming onto the market each year. It is no surprise that the enterprise prospered.

Although Schreiner died in 1931, his children Robert, Connie and Gus continued his work until disaster struck in the late 1930s. A series of severe winters killed off almost all their iris stock, amassed over many years, and the family took the decision to relocate the nursery to the more congenial climate of Salem, Oregon. Conditions in this region are ideal for irises, and the nursery continues to flourish today, still under family ownership.

Winner of the US Dykes Medal in 1992, 'Dusky Challenger' is one of the most important of the many exciting varieties of iris to emerge from the Schreiner nursery in recent years. When tightly furled in bud the glossy petals have a beetle-black character ('just as though they've been dipped in black ink', as one iris lover told me), but once fully open they assume the most opulent shade of deepest blue-purple, shimmering in the light and heavy on the hand, like a sort of iridescent cloth. Like indigo-dyed silk, in fact. Their large and ruffled shape emphasises this luxurious quality, and produces a spectacular rippling effect in breezy weather.

The same iris lover said that the overall effect of 'Dusky Challenger', its size, structure and colour, reminded him of formal evening wear and of 'getting ready for a good night out!'. This is indeed a very dressy plant, and one that should be savoured at leisure. It performs well in a border, and has a delicious scent, redolent of hot chocolate and tea-rooms on winter afternoons.

type: **tall bearded**
date: **1941**
grower: **Hall**
height: **90cm (36in)**
colour: **burgundy & yellow**
in flower: **early/mid-season**

Firecracker

Canadian-born David Hall was one of the great iris growers of the twentieth century. After a 44-year career with the American Telegraph and Telephone Company, he retired in 1940 and devoted his energies to rearing irises and hemerocallis (day-lilies). He raised thousands of iris seedlings every year, experimenting endlessly with a range of different lines, and although most famous for his flamingo pinks and 'large and shining' yellows, he was also particularly active with plicatas, ie varieties in which a pale ground colour – usually yellow or white – is overlaid with darker patterning. The first American plicata was 'True Charm', raised by Grace Sturtevant in 1917, and Hall was seminal in extending the range and variety of plicatas that were to follow in its wake, especially after the Second World War.

'Firecracker' is one of Hall's less well-known introductions, but nonetheless significant for that. In terms of coloration it is a precursor to later varieties such as the more famous 'Provençal' (see p.66), but what makes Firecracker so striking is its shape. This is very traditional, with elongated falls arching down and almost under, creating a stylised 'fleur-de-lys' profile with clean lines and symmetry throughout. The colours are rich and vibrant: the large standards an exuberant shade of flesh-red with a hint of bronze, the falls of lemon yellow spangled and edged in burgundy and with a delicate central line that bisects the blade. The beard is long, large and the colour of egg yolk.

In a plant-breeding career lasting nearly four decades, Hall introduced over 300 new varieties of iris and hemerocallis. He was quiet man, but widely acknowledged as one of the foremost iris experts anywhere. British irisarian Harry Randall commented after visiting Hall: 'He would just stand and gaze at them [his seedlings] without saying a word. At last I felt compelled to say to him, "If I had seedlings like that … I should do a backwards somersault, and yet you don't flicker an eyelid. Don't you feel excited about them?" At that his eyes twinkled and he replied, "Yes, I do, but my excitement is of the inward variety."' One of Hall's greatest achievements came in 1951, when his beautiful pink self, 'Cherie', won the US Dykes Medal. He was still actively involved with irises when, shortly before his 93rd birthday in 1968, he was tragically killed, struck down by a train whilst crossing the track near his home in Illinois.

type: **tall bearded**

date: **known by 16th century**

grower: **unknown**

height: **90cm (36in)**

colour: **white**

in flower: **early season**

Florentina

The elegant 'Florentina' was considered formerly to be a species iris. However, it is now recognised as a very old cultivar, possibly an albino variant of *I. germanica*, and is particularly celebrated for its role in the production of orris root. The importance of the latter in the worlds of medicine and cosmetics ensured the early presence of 'Florentina' in the gardens of monasteries and apothecaries. The flower was valued for its beauty and scent, and was soon welcomed into gardens for its aesthetic qualities alone. The predominant form is a creamy white colour, with a hint of iridescent blue throughout and a yellow beard. The falls are yellow on the haft, with olive veining, and have the 'hang dog' or 'cow's tongue' profile so characteristic of species bearded irises and older cultivars.

Although orris can be derived from the rhizomes of virtually all types of tall bearded iris, that of 'Florentina' is especially fragrant and was traditionally the most sought after, although *I. pallida* (*see* p.48) was more common and produced the bulk of the crop. The production of orris root was particularly established around the Italian city of Florence (*see* p.16), and iris fields were a common sight on the hillsides of Tuscany, where the planting and cultivation of irises was the source of much activity and, for some landowners and traders at least, considerable revenue. According to the herbalist Mrs Grieve: 'When the iris begins to grow, the ground is carefully and systematically weeded, this being done chiefly by the women, who traverse the rows of plants barefoot, hoeing up the weeds; whole families of peasants work at this, and in the subsequent collection, trimming and drying of the roots.' The rhizomes were not dug up until mature (ie three years old, on average), and were then peeled, sliced and dried in a warm, dark place for between twelve and eighteen months. Care was taken not to use fuel-fired heat, as the smell of woodsmoke or paraffin would ruin the orris scent. According to Mrs Grieve, roughly 1,000 tons of freshly dug rhizomes yielded some 300 tons of dried root.

The dried rhizomes were packed into casks if destined for export, or ground into powder for local use. This was used in the production of violet powders (which, ironically, have nothing to do with violets), an essential ingredient for the perfume industry. Used in pot pourri, ground orris can maintain its aroma for up to three years.

type: **tall bearded**
date: **1973**
grower: **Plough**
height: **95cm (38in)**
colour: **purple-black**
in flower: **mid-/late season**

Interpol

Black is the El Dorado of the plant world. Black tulips, black roses, black irises; they have all excited and challenged plant-breeders for centuries, and the quest for the purest black variety of each continues today. As far as irises are concerned, it is only in recent decades that the darkest shades of either blue or purple have become attainable. Much of the early work in this field was carried out by expert growers such as the Sass brothers (see 'The Black Douglas', p.32) and Paul Cook, another resident of the rural American Mid-West, who devoted many years of his life to iris hybridisation. In 1950 Cook registered the stunning dark purple self, 'Sable Night', which was to win the US Dykes Medal five years later. It was the blackest variety of its time, and one that other breeders strove to emulate and improve upon. It is a testament to its quality that it has remained popular ever since and continues to serve as a yardstick by which other dark irises are judged.

For me, 'Interpol' is one of the most out-standing black varieties available today. Sandwiched between the ground-breaking 'Sable Night' and the new crop of 'blacks' that has appeared in the last twenty years, it more than holds its own. It is positively funereal, the heavily sculpted petals giving it a highly distinctive profile and bringing to mind the heavy plush mourning garb of the Victorian age. The flower perches, raven-like, at the top of a tall and statuesque stem, whilst the petals are luxuriantly velvety, heavy to hold and with distinctive scalloped fringes, giving an overall crimped effect.

As with many so-called 'black' varieties of iris, 'Interpol' is in reality very dark purple and, as is also usually the case, the falls are a discernibly darker shade than the standards. The beard is purple with bronze tips, producing a speckled effect, and the buds and the base of the foliage are both flushed with a dark fuchsia pink. This all makes for a very superior plant indeed. Other stunning black varieties include the tall beardeds 'Before the Storm' (Innerst, 1989) and 'Black Tie Affair' (Schreiner, 1993), and the intermediate 'Langport Wren' (p.56).

type: **tall bearded**
date: **known by 16th century**
grower: **species iris**
height: **90cm (36in)**
colour: **pale mauve**
in flower: **early season**

Iris pallida

This species has played a seminal role in the development of irises. Indeed, along with *I. germanica* and *I. variegata*, it is the original parent of most modern cultivars, and in many senses all iris roads can be said to lead from these three species. *Pallida* is a native plant of the eastern Mediterranean, and although not indigenous to Italy it has been extensively naturalised there for many centuries. It grows readily on rocky ground and among patches of scrub, especially on south-facing hillsides and often in extensive clumps. From the earliest times it was used in gardens, and along with 'Florentina' (*see* p.44) traditionally formed the main source of the highly prized orris root. The robust habit and vigorous nature of *pallida* are two reasons why it has been so successful, both as a naturalised species and as a garden plant, where it can compete happily with most perennials.

The name *pallida* refers to the pale colour of the flower, a thin lavender blue or mauve. There also exists a rarer pink form. The species traditionally had other names, such as 'Pale Flag', 'Dalmatian Iris' (being particularly widespread in Dalmatia, or present-day Croatia) and 'Sweet Iris', on account of its deliciously fragrant scent. The flowers are modest in size, with rather compact, translucent petals and a bright yellow beard, and the plant flowers freely, often carrying six flowers per stem. The foliage is also attractive, the slightly glaucous leaves making this a particularly suitable species for planting in borders alongside silver-foliaged plants.

The ability of this species to maintain its long-standing place in our gardens has been enhanced further by the development of various cultivars, which although not blessed with especially distinguished flowers, certainly excel in their foliage. Notable among these is the stunning *I. pallida* 'Variegata', its leaves highlighted with broad cream stripes running along much of the leaf blade, and 'Argentea Variegata', where the stripes are white.

48

type:	**tall bearded**
date:	**1950**
grower:	**Graves**
height:	**90cm (36in)**
colour:	**powder blue**
in flower:	**mid-season**

Jane Phillips

'That old survivor, the Joan Collins of the iris world'. The verdict of an elderly Dorset gardener on 'Jane Phillips', and undeniably true. This seminal variety made its first appearance shortly after the end of the Second World War, yet over half a century later is still one of the most admired and popular of the blue varieties of tall bearded iris. Much of this success is due to the pure blueness of the flower, which is soft yet clear in tone and not suffused with the same extent of lilac as many of the other 'blue' varieties. Both standards and falls are elegantly veined, giving the characteristic 'crêpe paper' effect, and the strong and defined pale vanilla-white beard is immediately eye-catching. The large flowerhead holds a classic shape and represents a stage in the transition between the rather elongated forms of early twentieth-century varieties (with their pendulous falls and some-times undersized standards) and the squarer, more sym-metrical appearance of many modern cultivars.

Robust and disease-resistant, 'Jane Phillips' has attractive glaucous leaves and she is also notable for her exotic scent, heavily reminiscent of sherbet. These are both excellent reasons for planting this variety in a mixed border, as in the Rose Garden at Sissinghurst Castle (*below left*), where it is shown to great advantage adjacent to a large *Ceanothus*.

'Jane Phillips' was bred by Dr Robert J. Graves, an American doctor who served in the First World War. He developed a keen interest in irises after returning home to Concord, New Hampshire, and was especially fascinated by the blue and white forms, which he began hybridising in the 1930s. He introduced many new varieties to the market, including the splendid pale blue, 'Helen McGregor', which won the US Dykes Medal in 1949. Sadly, Graves died not long after 'Jane Phillips' was made widely available to the public, and so did not live to see her enduring success. However, other breeders have built on his work since then, using 'Jane Phillips' as a parent in the development of further award-winning var-ieties. Today, these cultivars can often be found growing in gardens alongside 'Jane Phillips', the latter remaining a yardstick against which other varieties are judged. In many respects, she remains unsurpassed.

type: **tall bearded**
date: **1960**
grower: **Murawska**
height: **90cm (36in)**
colour: **white**
in flower: **mid-season**

Juneau

Named after the state capital of Alaska, 'Juneau' is one of the unsung successes of the competitive world of the white iris. White irises have always been popular, and iris breeders have succeeded in developing a bewildering range of different shades and tones on the white theme, from ivory to milk to ice and beyond. This degree of variation has been matched by great ingenuity in the beard department, with yellow, orange, red, blue and white all now possible. Meanwhile, in line with tall bearded iris evolution generally, the petals of modern white selfs have become bigger, thicker and more ruffled, producing the more extravagant 'wedding-dress' style varieties of recent years.

'Skating Party', one of the most popular white cultivars.

In such a fast and frenzied world, understated style and restraint have great appeal. Cue 'Juneau'. With generous petals the colour of starched linen and a superb 'crêpe' texture, this variety has no need to resort to cleverly contrived tones or excessively fancy petal form to make its point. It is a great favourite of David Root at Kelways, one of the oldest iris nurseries in Britain: "Juneau' has a fabulous flower, brilliant in full sunshine. I particularly enjoy the tiny crinkles along the edges of the petals, like a rim of frost.' An iris of great presence and confidence, in some senses 'Juneau' continues the tradition established by earlier whites such as 'White City' (see p.90) and the now hardly known but quite stunning 'Whitehall' (see p.22).

The 1980s were a particular time of success with the hybridisation of white irises, and that decade spawned two of the most successful varieties of recent years: 'Skier's Delight' (Schreiner, 1982) and 'Skating Party' (Gaulter, 1983). The latter is a vigorous and extravagant affair, with large flowers of ivory white. It looks spectacular, flowers most freely and carries up to ten blooms per spike, each opening in turn to create an extended display. 'Juneau' cannot claim this last attribute, yet for me it still has the edge. Perhaps one needs to have them both in the garden.

Relatively little is known about A. L. Murawska, the grower of 'Juneau'. He lived in Illinois, home also to that great iris hybridiser, David Hall (see 'Firecracker', p.42). Along with 'Juneau', Murawska registered no fewer than six new varieties in 1960.

type: **intermediate bearded**
date: **not registered**
grower: **Kelways**
height: **45cm (18in)**
colour: **buff & pink**
in flower: **early/mid-season**

Langport Tartan

An unusually coloured variety, 'Langport Tartan' is one of a whole raft of intermediate irises introduced by Kelways nursery in Somerset. The nursery was established in 1851 by James Kelway, one of many individuals at that time who saw the opportunities offered by the rapidly expanding market for interesting plants, not just those imported from overseas but also new cultivars bred in the increasingly sophisticated systems of heated glasshouses and frames. Kelway's enterprise expanded rapidly, and he was soon employing over 400 staff and occupying more than 200 hectares (500 acres) of stock beds and glasshouses. Although the nursery became known primarily for its superb range of peonies, breeding increasingly exotic forms, it also developed a reputation for good-quality irises and issued its first dedicated iris catalogue in 1948. New seedlings were introduced each year, and this side of the business expanded as demand grew.

Intermediate irises have always been something of a British interest, with much of the pioneering work carried out by William Caparne (see p.38). As the American growers concentrated on developing the form and colour permutations of the tall bearded iris, so breeders like Kelways' owners Owen Lloyd and his son John focused on expanding the colour range of the intermediates. Some 80 new varieties of the latter were introduced by the Lloyds during the 1960s and '70s, and they were characterised by the addition of the 'Langport' prefix to their name, after the nearby market town and erstwhile inland port. Many of these proved highly popular with gardeners, and several are still available commercially (see 'Langport Wren', p.56).

Introduced in 1972 but never officially registered, 'Langport Tartan' is an intriguing mix of colours. The standards are pale buff, with a pinkish flush at the base, whilst the falls are a beguiling mix of deep rose pink and bronze. Highly distinctive is the dark flecking that appears on the petals; these marks are caused by a genetic virus, endemic to the variety but not, it appears, transmittable to other cultivars or species. The flecking is unique to each bloom and hugely variable, from the barely discernible in some cases to others in which it almost dominates the petals. Purists would discard 'Langport Tartan' on these grounds alone, but for me it adds further interest to what is an already attractive variety. Who would want manufactured perfection in a plant anyway?

type: **intermediate bearded**

date: **1995**

grower: **Kelways**

height: **65cm (26in)**

colour: **deep magenta**

in flower: **early/mid-season**

Langport Wren

This is perhaps the most famous of the intermediate irises introduced by Kelways in the 1970s, although it was not registered until nearly two decades later. Now deservedly appreciated for its rich colouring, profusely flowering habit and vigorous growth, it is a popular and widespread variety, and certainly in the top flight of the darker cultivars.

The large, round petals of 'Langport Wren' are striking, both standards and falls being almost fan-like in shape. Their colour is an endless source of attraction, and varies quite widely, depending on light conditions and the age of the bloom. In dull weather the flower can appear almost matt black, with heavy, velvet-like petals that are flared and lightly crimped along the edges. The arrival of sunshine brings to life a new plant entirely, with the sensual magenta flush of the petals becoming prominent. This is particularly so on the standards, which take on a vibrant, silky quality in bright light and glitter like amethyst when caught by the sun. The falls are more consistently darker, but with attractive mid-magenta striation discernible on the haft, immediately beneath the beard. The latter is dark brown, the ends bleached with tawny ginger; it is arguably the most convincing of the 'tiger-moth caterpillar' type of iris beard.

Peerless among the darker intermediates, this is regarded as one of the best garden irises of any colour. In recognition of this fact it was granted an Award of Garden Merit by the Royal Horticultural Society in 1998. AGMs are awarded to plants that meet certain criteria related to their constitution, availability, resistance to disease and pests, ease of growth, genetic stability and – most pertinent of all – ability to perform well in the garden context. An award is only made after stringent trials or detailed observation of the plant in action. It is little surprise that 'Langport Wren' passed such tests; this is a quality iris, and one worthy of incorporation into any garden. The gilt on this particular lily is its scent: a rich chocolate-orange fragrance.

type: **tall bearded**
date: **1933**
grower: **Murrell**
height: **104cm (41in)**
colour: **rose pink & lilac**
in flower: **mid-season**

London Pride

'You can have a complete garden with Irises alone, but you cannot have a complete garden without them. When you have bought an Iris you have furnished your garden permanently.' So claims the introduction to the 1953 catalogue of the Orpington Nurseries Company, established in the 1920s by Percy and Olive Murrell in what was then a small Kent market town just outside London. Major Percy Murrell was a keen horticulturalist and the son of a famous rose grower, and after service in the First World War he turned his attentions to the commercial rearing of irises and general nursery stock. The Murrells' nursery flourished and became renowned internationally for the quality and range of its irises. The couple became leading lights in the British Iris Society and regularly travelled to France to keep abreast of developments at the various specialist nurseries there (see 'Béotie', p.28).

The Murrells were conscientious hybridisers, introducing many new forms of iris to supplement those on their stocklist that were imported from overseas suppliers. Sadly, very few of these cultivars are available commercially today, which is surprising in view of the beauty of many of the varieties developed at Orpington. Among these was 'London Pride', a stunning pink bicolour which made a huge impact when first shown at the Chelsea Flower Show in 1933. It is very tall, with well-branched stems and large flowers of superb shape and colour. The standards, described in the 1933 Orpington catalogue as 'a rosy cyclamen' are perhaps rather more lilac in tone, but undoubtedly strong and well formed. The falls are a deeper colour, straight-hanging and are slightly waved at the edges. The beard is medium yellow on white, and the flower has a delicious fragrance.

'London Pride' can be seen at its decorative best in the rose garden at Sissinghurst Castle in Kent, where it is also valued for its height and freely flowering nature. It must rank as one of the Murrells' most notable successes; Major Murrell died in 1942, but his wife continued to run their nursery until her own death in 1957 (see also 'White City', p.90).

type: **tall bearded**
date: **1942**
grower: **Schreiner**
height: **90cm (36in)**
colour: **blue & purple**
in flower: **mid-/late season**

Lothario

Named after the hero of Nicholas Rowe's 1703 tragedy *Fair Penitent* ('Is this that haughty gallant, gay Lothario?'), and carrying a name that has passed into the English language as a term for a playboy or womaniser, 'Lothario' is an iris of great character and presence. It has a superb profile, with generous standards of a mid-violet blue and falls of rich purple arching steeply down. Today, of course, such a traditional shape and form might be regarded as dated – some would criticise the relative size of the falls to the standards, for example – but 'Lothario' was very much the product of its time, and in the 1940s and early '50s its elegance and colour combination were a justifiable source of pleasure and excitement.

In the years immediately after the end of the Second World War, American growers made great strides in the hybridisation of new varieties of tall bearded iris, and most British irisarians looked across the Atlantic for the most up-to-date trends and colour innovations. The Orpington Nurseries catalogue of 1953 lists 'Lothario' as one of 'the latest novelties and introductions from America', and Kelways described it in the same year as 'a very fine iris'. It was described initially as a superior type of 'blue bi-color' (the latter being an iris in which the standards and falls are different colours and the term blue being applied loosely to everything from lavender to purple), but in today's terms would be classed as a neglecta, ie a variety with pale blue standards and dark blue or purple falls. Either way, it was immediately appreciated, both in its own right and as a variety similar to – and arguably an improvement on – the famous 'Sir Michael' (Yeld, 1925), a popular iris in the late 1920s and '30s. 'Lothario' represented the new generation and, rather appropriately given its name, served as a parent in the hybridisation of the next crop of new irises (see 'Braithwaite', p.36).

'Lothario' plays an important role in the purple border of the top courtyard at Sissinghurst, where Vita Sackville-West created what was probably the first major border to be composed entirely of purple and magenta plants. Former head gardener Sarah Cook explains: 'The purple border is ranged in front of a brick wall, and so we rely on tall plants such as irises to give some height and poise without obscuring the texture behind. 'Lothario' is perfect for this, those rich colours working so well against terracotta. To my mind it is one of the most elegant irises of all.'

type: **tall bearded**
date: **1844**
grower: **Lémon**
height: **90cm (36in)**
colour: **violet plicata**
in flower: **mid-season**

Madame Chéreau

One of many varieties released onto the market by the French plantsman Lémon during the 1840s (*see* p.22), 'Madame Chéreau' was named after the wife of the President of the Cercle Général d'Horticulture in Paris at the time. One of the earliest plicatas, it quickly became popular as both a feature plant in formal planting schemes and, later, as a decorative component in the increasingly fashionable herbaceous border. It soon became an established variety, offered by most of the leading nurseries, including that of Amos Perry at Enfield, Middlesex, who described it as 'extremely pretty' and 'one of the best'. At 6d per plant it was good value, and considerably cheaper than many other varieties. Very free-flowering, the plant has tall, strong stems and is generally disease-resistant, unlike many of its contemporaries, which were notoriously vulnerable to infection, pests and inclement weather.

The coloration is quite superb, the ivory white petals exquisitely marked with the finest violet stitching around the edges of both standards and falls. The regularity and precision of this pencilling effect exceeds that of many subsequent plicatas, and is enhanced by the small size of the flowerheads. The squarish falls are strong and defined and the standards well sculpted and proportionate, producing a solid and compact impression. The blade of the falls is flushed with vanilla, enhancing the delicate white beard, the tips of which are brushed with yellow.

Deborah Evans, head gardener at the National Trust's Tyntesfield, an extravagant Victorian Gothic house near Bristol, is a fervent admirer: 'For me, 'Madame Chéreau' is one of the most beautiful of all irises. It has an intricate beauty about it that perfectly evokes its heyday in the elaborate and labour-intensive gardens of the Victorian and Edwardian eras. This is particularly relevant at Tyntesfield, where we are currently researching the origins and development of the formal flowerbeds. Here the re-planting of antique iris varieties such as 'Madame Chéreau' and 'Queen of May' [see p.70] may be both appropriate historically and very successful visually.'

type: **dwarf bearded**
date: **1991**
grower: **Blyth**
height: **36cm (14in)**
colour: **peach & pink**
in flower: **early season**

Melodic

Dwarf bearded irises are the smallest of the three main groups of bearded iris. Also known as lilliput irises, they grow between 20 and 41cm (8–16in) and flower earlier than their intermediate and tall brethren. Most varieties are in bloom between late April and mid- or late May, and the range of colour combinations available today reflects the proliferation of different shades and tones that have obsessed breeders of the tall bearded iris for many decades.

The first dwarf iris cultivars appeared on the market in the early years of the twentieth century and many can look to *I. pumila*, a native plant across southern and eastern Europe, for their provenance. Iris breeders were drawn to this species by its high degree of natural variation (it may in fact be an ancient natural hybrid) and they crossed it with other similar species and existing cultivars to create new varieties. These are generally taller and more robust than their ancestors, although the form is consistent.

The rich, jewel colouring of the dwarf bearded iris, 'Tarheel Elf'.

Dwarf varieties have only small branches on their flower-spike, and so each plant usually carries only two or three flowers. However, they are valued by gardeners for their rapid rate of proliferation and, being shorter and more compact, for their greater resistance to wind, the scourge of taller irises. They are also less dependent on direct sunlight, so vital for the ripening of the larger varieties. In terms of planting, dwarf irises are particularly effective at the front of a border or in a rock garden, and in recent years their popularity has grown hugely, no doubt linked in part to the current vogue for gravel gardens, in which dwarf irises will usually prosper.

'Melodic' is an outstanding variety, with a fresh and confident air. The standards are a sensual flesh-pink, smoked with peach, and the falls notable for their stunning 'thumbprint' (a characteristic of many dwarf bearded varieties), in this case of cerise fringed with mauve and with a hint of blue in the centre. A pale blue beard and attractive tiger-stripe markings on the hafts complete what is, in every sense, the perfect springtime plant.

type: **tall bearded**
date: **1977**
grower: **Cayeux**
height: **85cm (34in)**
colour: **burgundy & yellow**
in flower: **early/mid-season**

Provençal

One of the most striking plicatas and a highly rated variety by plantsmen and gardeners alike. Awarded the title of 'L'Iris du Millénaire' in 2000, this is a plant with real poise, the petals neat and trim, beautifully in proportion, both to each other and the overall scale of the plant, and with no ruffling or overblown frills. They have a firm texture, maintaining their shape well and appearing prolifically on long, elegant stems above grey-green foliage.

'Provençal' bud, showing the dramatic coloration and patterning.

The colour combination is unusual and dramatic. Deep burgundy-brown predominates, saturating the standards and providing the framework for the exquisite falls. These are of primrose yellow, with a tawny-orange beard on a white bed and a Milky Way of maroon flecking spilling over the rest of the petal. A thin line of flecks converges to form a vertical stripe down the centre of each fall, creating the characteristic 'baby's bottom' effect. The flower is heavily scented, and redolent of orange blossom.

There is something about 'Provençal' that makes one think of roses. Perhaps this is prompted by the rounded shape of the falls and the compact flowerhead. The velvet texture of the standards certainly reminds me of the fabulous rose 'Louis Quatorze', and produces the same sensual effect. Overall, however, the success of 'Provençal' is perhaps due more to its restraint than anything else. This is an iris that has succeeded in a world of more ostentatious cultivars because of its solid quality: a stylish and balanced shape, great colours and a superb scent.

'Provençal' was developed by the Cayeux nursery in France, which has been hybridising and introducing new varieties of iris for little short of a century. Established by Ferdinand Cayeux (see 'Béotie', p.28), the nursery was rejuvenated after the Second World War by his son, René, and was moved to its present location at Gien in the Loire Valley by René's son, Jean. Here he established an international reputation for his iris breeding, and his work continues today under the stewardship of his son, Richard (see also 'Vive la France', p.86).

type: **intermediate bearded**
date: **1909**
grower: **Farr**
height: **70cm (27in)**
colour: **pink, bronze & blue**
in flower: **late season**

Quaker Lady

One of the best known and appreciated of what are now known as the 'historic irises', 'Quaker Lady' was bred by the American Bertrand Farr and achieved star status soon after he introduced it to the market in 1909. Farr was originally a music store owner in Wyomissing, Pennsylvania, but was also a keen amateur gardener. As the plant bug bit, he gradually wound up his music business and opened a nursery, launching his new enterprise with an upbeat marketing drive, the like of which had never been seen before in plant circles. By using colour plates in his catalogue, the first time this had been attempted on such a scale, he was able to present potential customers with a lifelike representation of his plants. This proved to be a masterstroke, and he was soon selling irises in large quantities, despite charging what was considered a prohibitive price at the time: 75 cents per pot. Regarded as the 'premier American iris' of its day, 'Quaker Lady' was quickly among his bestsellers.

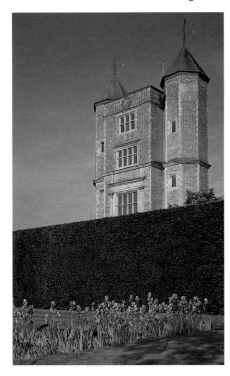

'The Lady', as this variety was affectionately known, has one of the most sensual of all colour combinations. Dykes called it 'curious', but did not deny its appeal and beauty. The pale pink standards are tinged with bronze and matched against deep lilac falls shot with blue, producing a smoky lavender effect. The bright wax-coloured beard stands out well, and the veining on the olive and yellow-flushed haft provides definition and impact. The leaves have an attractive purple flush at their base. A vigorous and free-flowering variety, it has a solid shape and appearance, and the petals are well proportioned. Ideal for blended use in the herbaceous border, especially when set with yellows, 'Quaker Lady' also performs well as a feature plant. It is particularly effective in the orchard at Sissinghurst Castle Garden in Kent, where it has been planted in a rather formal manner around the brick paving that marks the foundations of the old house (*see left*).

type: **intermediate bearded**
date: **pre-1859**
grower: **Salter**
height: **65cm (25in)**
colour: **lilac & rose pink**
in flower: **late season**

Queen of May

This enchanting old iris has very special appeal. A beautiful combination of pale lilac standards and rose pink falls with subtle magenta striations, it flowers freely and creates a fabulous pink flush when planted *en masse*.

Gertrude Jekyll, the celebrated garden designer, had a particular fondness for 'Queen of May'. She used it in her own garden at Munstead Wood near Godalming in Surrey, as well as in the planting schemes she prepared for her many clients across the country. A leading advocate of a naturalistic approach to planting, Miss Jekyll espoused a carefully crafted approach to colour, texture and height, seamlessly weaving together many different types of plant into an apparently 'natural' ensemble. She adored irises, although using them in a herbaceous border was not straightforward. As early bloomers they tended to flower before all of Miss Jekyll's favoured companion plants were fully out, leaving

'colour gaps' and upsetting the carefully chosen harmony of the entire scheme. The late-flowering nature of 'Queen of May' made it ideal for such situations, and so Miss Jekyll used it extensively. It certainly featured in the dramatic iris and lupin border she created at Munstead Wood, in which blue, white, yellow and pink irises combined with various lupins to create a frothing sea of blooms. She also valued 'Queen of May' as a companion to roses, rightly identifying its delicate pink flower as the perfect complement to China roses such as *Rosa X odorata* 'Pallida'.

One of Miss Jekyll's most renowned successes with irises was at Barrington Court in Somerset, where she was consulted on the planting scheme for a new garden shortly after the end of the First World War. As part of a wider series of 'compartments', she designed – without ever visiting the site, her ideas based on photographs and soil samples – a stunning rose and iris garden, in which 'Queen of May' featured and which is now being re-created by the National Trust.

type: **tall bearded**
date: **1968**
grower: **Smith**
height: **very variable**
colour: **ivory & burgundy**
in flower: **early / late season**

Repartee

This is a particularly handsome variety and intriguing for all sorts of reasons. Now regarded as an 'historic', 'Repartee' has been available commercially for over three decades and has remained popular since its introduction. Few new varieties have come close to the simple, dramatic effect created by its colour combination, the latter being one of the few certainties about this plant.

Julian Browse, owner of Seagate Irises, a specialist nursery in the bleak hinterland of the Lincolnshire/Norfolk border, knows 'Repartee' well: 'What I like so much about it is its temperament. It's so fickle and variable. Some years it grows tall, in others it comes up shorter. One year it will rebloom, the next you get only one flush. You never know where you are with it.' Such extreme contrariness is unusual in irises, but 'Repartee' has perfected the art of unpredictability. Even established plants will vary in height year on year, responding – but never consistently – to variations in temperature and rainfall patterns. Shorter plants have a bunched-up habit, the plentiful buds tightly clustered, whilst taller individuals (which can reach 85cm/35in or so) have well-spaced blooms and are as elegant as

any of the more dependable tall bearded varieties. Even its rate of growth defies logical analysis; a group of plants growing next to each other will all increase at different rates, some vigorously, others hardly at all.

For most gardeners, however, the appeal of this iris resides in its arresting flower. The crisp, well-formed standards are of pale ivory flushed at the base with primrose yellow, the flared falls a blend of deep terracotta and burgundy, the latter predominant in the centre of the petal and with a contrasting ivory fringe defining the slightly waved profile of the petal. The hafts are lightly striated, and the beard yellow.

As for flowering, capricious 'Repartee' can bloom at any time between mid-May and late June, then again – if the mood takes it – in August or September. Most remontant irises, ie those that rebloom later in the season, are erratic in this sense, and this has tended to hamper their commercial appeal. North American breeders in particular have worked to develop more reliable reblooming varieties, and the range and dependability of those cultivars offering two flowerings a year is constantly expanding.

type: **tall bearded**
date: **1934**
grower: **Pilkington**
height: **90cm (36in)**
colour: **yellow**
in flower: **mid-season**

Sahara

'An aristocrat in every way', proclaimed one nursery catalogue, when first introducing this variety to its customers in 1936. Winner of the British Dykes Medal the previous year, 'Sahara' was acclaimed for its 'clear colouring, perfect form and great refinement'. It was bred by Geoffrey Pilkington, a founder member of the British Iris Society, to which he devoted many years of service as president and honorary secretary. He was a man of firm and fast decisions: at the outbreak of war in 1940 he decided to reduce his iris collection to just 50 varieties but, rather oddly given its prize-winning status, did not include 'Sahara' among them. Then, in 1950, he abandoned bearded irises altogether upon discovering that the garden of his new home was prone to leaf spot, turning instead to conifers and rhododendrons for solace.

A superb primrose yellow, 'Sahara' has a warm buff blush near the base of its petals, which are beautifully shaped and construct a distinguished profile. The standards are strong and arched, the falls slightly flared and delicately waved at the edges, with elegant buff veining running their full length. The beard is golden and there is an elegant citrus fragrance. With well-branched stems and vigorous growth, this variety was particularly well regarded for its garden effect, a pure yellow self being much easier to weave into the colour palette of an intricate flower border than some of the more complicated varieties on the market at the time.

Why, given all these attributes, is 'Sahara' such a rare find today? It may not be commercially available at all in the United Kingdom at present, and few gardens are still blessed by it. One of these is at Myddelton House in Enfield on the edge of London, the former home of the great plantsman E. A. Bowles and where the national collection of award-winning bearded irises is now held. Christine Murphy, head gardener, treasures its presence there: 'This lovely old iris was around in Mr Bowles's time. Its subtle colour and simple flower shape are quite beautiful and a great foil to many other plants; apart from maintaining it in the collection we also use it in a mixed border. It's such a shame that it is not more widely grown.'

type: **tall bearded**
date: **1932**
grower: **Neel**
height: **100cm (40in)**
colour: **pink & purple**
in flower: **late season**

Shah Jehan

Pure exoticism, this iris has attracted more than its fair share of plaudits since appearing on the market in the early 1930s. The terms 'sensational', 'striking' and 'extravaganza' – all three were used to describe it in Schreiner's 1942 catalogue – hardly do it justice. It is a more subtle and powerful collection of colours than at first sight, and thus repays careful contemplation. Indeed, so varied and complex are the shades and tones of its petals that a detailed description can never be anything more than purely subjective. The standards are a pale creamy white flushed with lavender, with a warm buff hue at the base. The falls are decidedly opulent, of velvet plum suffused in mahogany and with sensual pale pink edges. The rich yellow beard sits upon a firework display of striations and contours.

If such colours were not enough, this is a tall, robust and late-flowering iris, and one that can more than hold its own in a mixed bed. Certainly an iris of royal rank, and deservedly named after one of the most celebrated of the Mughal emperors. The Mughals knew and enjoyed irises, and iris motifs were carved commonly into their palaces and forts (see p.11). Shah Jehan ruled from 1627 to 1658 and is best known for the building of the Taj Mahal, dedicated to his beloved wife, Mumtaz Mahal, and itself adorned with floral imagery.

In addition to sustaining and developing the floral decorative style so espoused by his father, Jahangir, Shah Jehan also took the Mughals' love of gardens to new heights through his creation of the Shalamar Gardens in Lahore (now Pakistan). This elaborate complex of water features, pavilions and niches full of flowers was completed in 1642 and represents the apogee of the Mughal quest to bring something of the paradise gardens of Kashmir down to the flat plains of greater India. A creation of sublime beauty, it was arguably as significant a legacy to mankind as the Taj. Sadly, Shah Jehan's cultural and artistic endeavours cost him dear; although imperial revenues went up greatly during his reign, they were exceeded by royal expenditure, and the emperor's extravagant quest for beauty and power sowed the seeds for what would be a protracted decline for the Mughal dynasty. Today, the Shalamar Gardens are both a popular social venue in Lahore and a UNESCO World Heritage Site, albeit one in urgent need of sensitive restoration.

type: **tall bearded**
date: **1940**
grower: **Pillow**
height: **102cm (40in)**
colour: **yellow & maroon**
in flower: **mid-/late season**

Shannopin

This striking variety was among those selected in 1961 by Harold Nicolson for introduction into the garden which he created with his wife, Vita Sackville-West, at Sissinghurst in Kent. Irises were used skilfully by Harold and Vita to contrast with the famous roses there, and seldom have so many varieties of iris been planted so effectively in such a mixed and varied environment. 'Shannopin' is used dramatically alongside one of the flagstone paths in the rose garden, right in the front of the border and facing a stand of 'London Pride' (*below, and see* p.58). For many visitors their introduction to the rose garden is the colourful sight of the massed spikes of 'Shannopin' straining forward to greet them as they enter through the gate from the top courtyard.

Its drooping, rectangular falls give 'Shannopin' a decidedly old-fashioned shape and in some respects it must have seemed rather dated, even at the time of its introduction. Yet it produces tall and well-branched stems with many flowers, and although not large, these carry a most attractive colour combination, with primrose yellow standards and rich mulberry falls. Both colours tend to fade under strong sunlight, muting into delightful pastel shades. The haft is heavily striated with murrey on yellow, the patterning extending over one quarter to one third of the entire petal area and creating an attractive contrast when seen from afar. The Orpington Nurseries catalogue of 1953 refers to this variety as 'a striking and original iris, with great carrying power'. It is certainly a noticeable plant in any garden, and the yellow standards can be successful in lightening areas of darker planting.

'Shannopin' was named after the Native American town of the same name, a late seventeenth-century fur-trading post and the location of modern Pittsburgh, Pennsylvania. Its grower, T. Lloyd Pillow, was superintendent of the city's Street and Sewer Department.

type: **tall bearded**
date: **unknown**
grower: **unknown**
height: **90cm (36in)**
colour: **pink**
in flower: **mid-season**

'Sissinghurst Mystery'

This cultivar is something of an enigma. It grows in the rose garden at Sissinghurst Castle, alongside several other irises, including 'London Pride' (p.58), 'Shannopin' (p.78) and 'White City' (p.90). Until recently it was – incorrectly – labelled 'Rosy Veil', actually a violet plicata bred by Sass in 1953 (see photograph on p.34). The provenance of this pink self, and how it came to be at Sissinghurst, is not known, and further research is required to try to establish its real identity.

The shape and style of the flower are rather traditional, and typical of cultivars bred in the late 1940s and early '50s. In the view of one British Iris Society expert, it has the look of an American-bred iris, and in some respects it does indeed recall the 'flamingo pinks' bred by David Hall (see p.42) at that time. Its habits are not remarkable; Sarah Cook, Sissinghurst's former head gardener, reports that it 'is neither very free-flowering, nor a very good doer, but definitely rather lovely and unusual'. Certainly it has the most ravishing colour, a rich prawn pink, flushed with shades of magenta and with a full and bright orange beard. The falls are very slightly darker than the standards.

'Mystery' irises are surprisingly commonplace, with the precise identification of bearded iris cultivars often difficult and sometimes impossible. Without the chance of direct comparison with a labelled plant of certain and documented provenance, the chances of reaching a positive conclusion can be negligible. This is particularly so with historic irises, many of which are no longer commercially available, having fallen out of fashion. Some older cultivars have disappeared completely, whilst others languish forgotten in out-of-the-way corners of older gardens. Consequently, familiarity with certain cultivars, even among iris experts, can be very limited. In the case of 'Sissinghurst Mystery' we can only hope that exposure to a wider audience through inclusion in this book may help shed light on its real identity.

type: **tall bearded**
date: **1989**
grower: **Byers**
height: **105cm (41in)**
colour: **tan, cream & purple**
in flower: **late season**

Thornbird

This unusually coloured variety belongs to the 'space-agers', a group of irises in which particular features have been deliberately bred to what are considered, in the opinion of some, to be extreme limits. Repeated crossing can make possible the enhancement of individual aspects of an iris flowerhead. This is especially so with the beard, and one of the most common achievements is the development of a horn, effectively the rib that extends from the base of the beard, which is bred to rear up and stand proud above the blade of the fall.

Winner of the US Dykes Medal in 1997, 'Thornbird' is a rather bizarre affair. It boasts a

long purple horn that extends from under a full and furry ginger beard, and has petals of intriguing colours, rarely seen together in other cultivars. According to iris authority Geoff Stebbings, the overall colour of the flower was described by its grower, Monty Byers of California,

as 'écru', the French for raw or unbleached. Certainly there is something about the colour of the falls that can, in dull light, look rather sullied, reminiscent perhaps of tarnished bronze. In bright conditions, however, this is a most handsome variety, with flushes of purple on the hafts and with crisp cream standards, veined in lime-green and with considerable poise. This is a tall plant, often topping a metre or more in height and yet which holds its shape well in bad weather.

Space-age irises were first exploited commercially in the 1970s, and were apparently named because of the prevailing space exploration culture of the day. However, it is tempting to conclude that the term can be applied equally well to the more outlandish results of their hybridisation. This has attracted – and, indeed, continues to attract – criticism from those who regard such crossing as unethical and the results as mutants. For others, they represent innovation and variety. Either way, the practice is not without its drawbacks. Excessively bred features can be genetically inconsistent, and can fail to appear on every plant or every bloom, although in the case of 'Thornbird' the horn is invariably present.

type: **tall bearded**
date: **1929**
grower: **Cayeux**
height: **100cm (40in)**
colour: **burgundy & bronze**
in flower: **mid-season**

Vert Galant

'Vert Galant' belongs to an important group of irises that caused considerable excitement in the iris world when they were first introduced to the market during the late 1920s and '30s. Now regarded as decidedly old-fashioned, all of these varieties carry the same basic colour pattern of burgundy-red falls and pink or bronze/copper standards. They include 'Maréchal (or 'Mareschal') Ney' (Williamson, 1930), named after the famous French military commander who played a gallant role in Napoleon's ill-fated Russian Campaign of 1812. This cultivar was mentioned by Vita Sackville-West in her book *In Your Garden* (1951) as one of the 'reddish' varieties she valued. If she grew it in her garden at Sissinghurst Castle then it has not lasted, for there is no sign of it there today. Other similar varieties are the famous 'Alcazar', grown by Vilmorin in 1910, 'Dauntless', winner of the US Dykes Medal in 1929, and two other Cayeux introductions, 'Député Nomblot', winner of the French Dykes Medal in 1930, and 'Louvois', plus any number of other variations of the same general theme.

'Vert Galant' is typical of this group for having distinctive and generous veining on its falls. This feature was very popular in the early decades of the twentieth century but was viewed by many later breeders as undesirable striation and by some as an outright flaw. Concerted attempts were made to suppress it or breed it out altogether. This seems harsh; to less obsessive eyes the veining is attractive, and in 'Vert Galant' can take on an explosive quality, white arcs streaming across the rich burgundy of the fall like spilt milk across a red carpet. This creates a dramatic effect, and one that is enhanced by the generous yellow beard and the bronzed pink standards, strong and erect and with an attractive frosted texture. 'Vert Galant' also has another card to play: its height. Although typically a metre high, the flower-spikes of established plants can reach 120cm (47in), making this one of the tallest of the historic iris cultivars.

'Maréchal Ney' is an attractive but now very scarce old cultivar.

type: **tall bearded**
date: **1991**
grower: **Cayeux**
height: **90cm (36in)**
colour: **white & blue**
in flower: **mid-/late season**

Vive la France

The iris nursery established by Ferdinand Cayeux at Petit-Vitry (see pp.22, 28 and 84) is now based at Gien, some 80 miles (125kms) south of Paris, and flourishes today under the management of his great-grandson, Richard. It has continued to introduce an impressive range of new varieties and has developed an increasingly diverse range of amoenas, of which 'Vive la France' is one of the most striking.

An amoena is an iris with white standards and coloured falls. The oldest date back to the 1930s and the time of the renowned 'Wabash' (Williamson, 1936), a white and violet amoena and winner of the US Dykes Medal in 1940. The early amoenas tended to have blue or purple falls, but a greatly expanded palette has been developed in recent years and now includes copper-red, golden yellow and apricot pink. 'Vive la France' carries the more traditional colour combination, but with the well-branched, floriferous structure of modern irises, and with generous, ruffled petals.

Amoenas have a distinctive look: crisp and clean, with the consistently white standards serving as a 'screen' against which the richness of the coloured falls can be displayed to best advantage. In the case of 'Vive la France', this effect is heightened by the incandescent red beard, perhaps the reddest of any variety. The standards are clinically white, the large, rounded falls a bright indigo blue, with a central white heart showcasing the brilliant beard. The presence of this heart, with the haft markings radiating outwards, creates a sort of plicata effect, leading some iris authorities to claim that this variety is not a true amoena at all.

'Vive la France' is named in acknowledgement of its colour combination, the red-white-blue of the French national flag. It is one of a suite of similar varieties bred in the 1990s by Jean Cayeux, all of which demonstrate the same general colours and form, but with subtle variations. Of these, 'Vive la France' is the most vibrant, although the cooler, more restrained tones of 'Rebecca Perret' (1992) are equally irresistible.

type: **tall bearded**
date: **1992**
grower: **Schreiner**
height: **95cm (38in)**
colour: **brownish red**
in flower: **mid-season**

War Chief

The quest for a truly red iris has fascinated iris growers for many decades. Red is not a naturally occurring colour in iris genes, and any 'red' cultivars have, to date, always been impaired by the presence of brown or purple tones, creating a chestnut or burgundy effect. Yet whilst it is fair to say that a pure scarlet or crimson iris has still not been achieved, in recent years a range of new cultivars has come closer than ever before to this elusive goal. 'War Chief' has as strong a claim as any, and is a striking and compelling plant.

The flower is huge, with the heavy, slightly ruffled petals typical of modern varieties and a rather fleshy appearance overall. The standards are the colour of ripe watermelon, complete with a 'wet', slightly frosted quality. They are richly veined, and their shape and posture reminiscent of fan coral. The flared falls are also pink-red, but with a swathe of claret spilling down and across them, dark enough in places for the silky texture of the petal to reveal itself as a silver sheen. The beard is golden, spun with copper. This is one of the most prolifically flowering varieties of all, with four branches often carrying between eleven and thirteen buds in total, and its robust structure makes it a good performer in wet and windy weather. A further important quality is the resistance of its petals to fading or bleaching under strong sunlight or heavy rainfall.

'War Chief' was bred by the American nursery, Schreiner's (see p.40), which has played an important role in the recent evolution of red cultivars and the race to achieve a 'fire-engine' red. A wide range of red-related varieties has been developed there, many with interesting carmine and cranberry-coloured attributes. Two of the most impressive recent introductions have been 'Dynamite' (1997), with truly massive flowers of 12cm x 17cm (4¼in x 6¾in), and 'Ruby Morn' (2002), a deep ox-blood red.

type: **tall bearded**
date: **1939**
grower: **Murrell**
height: **104cm (41in)**
colour: **white with blue flush**
in flower: **mid-season**

White City

The famous Orpington Nurseries Company, better known simply as Orpington Irises (see p.58), arguably reached the pinnacle of its achievement with the introduction of this splendid variety, winner of the British Dykes Medal in 1940.

By the late 1930s Major Murrell was playing a less active role in the running of the nursery, and his wife, Olive, took over most of the responsibilities, including that for hybridisation. 'White City' was one of the results, although she registered and named no fewer than 92 different seedlings in total! Having left the strenuous regime of the Women's Land Army during the First World War, she sought the gentler pastures of a company of carnation-growers. This marked the beginning of a lifelong interest in plants, and Olive Murrell soon gained an international reputation as 'a walking encyclopaedia of irises', her advice and opinions sought on a regular basis. Although a woman of forthright views, she did not stint on encouraging the novice or amateur grower and was peerless in her ability to recognise and recall the names of hundreds of different, and often confusing, varieties.

A source of much pride to Mrs Murrell, 'White City' was considered the best white self yet grown at that time. The flowers are huge, and have a faint flush of lavender blue – 'plumbago blue', according to the Orpington catalogue of 1941 – when first opened. This is especially apparent on the standards, which are beautifully arched and create a delightful cradling effect when fresh. The falls are slightly flared and smooth, with delicate ginger veining at the very base of the haft and a white, yellow-tipped beard. Although described as 'sweetly scented' in the Orpington catalogue, in my experience the fragrance of 'White City' is not particularly notable. However, its other attributes are more than adequate to make this a superb plant. This is just as well, as when first released it cost 30s per pot, the equivalent of £50 in today's values.

White City was immediately a triumph, both in Britain and the United States. In many senses it was the last gasp of British iris growers before the Second World War took real hold and energies were understandably directed into other, more pressing matters. This opened the gate for American growers to take the lead in iris breeding for the next decade and beyond.

Glossary

Amoena   An iris with white or very pale standards and darker-coloured falls, usually of blue or purple

Beard   The hairy or bushy linear feature that runs down the centre of each fall, serving to attract pollinators to the inside of the flower

Bicolour   An iris in which the standards and falls are different colours

Bitone   An iris in which the standards and falls are different shades of the same colour

Blade   The central, flat surface of a petal

Cultivar   A cultivated variety of plant, usually a hybrid

Fall   The three outer petals of an iris, which open to reveal the standards and then either become horizontal or hang down vertically

Haft   The area of the fall closest to the centre of the flower; often marked with striations

Historic   The term given to an iris bred more than thirty years ago

Horn   A protuberance extending from the beard on 'space-age' irises

Neglecta   An iris with pale blue standards and darker blue or purple falls

Plicata   An iris with a white or very pale background colour, edged or 'stitched' in a darker colour

Remontant   An iris that blooms twice in one season

Self   An iris in which all the petals are of the same colour

'Space-age'   The term given to an iris bred with features extending from its beard, most notably a horn

Standard   The three inner petals of an iris which are contained within the falls when in bud, but once open are held vertically

Gardens with Notable Collections of Bearded Irises

Barrington Court (NT), near Ilminster, Somerset

Blickling Hall (NT), near Aylsham, Norfolk

British Iris Society Garden at the Royal National Rose Society's 'Garden of the Rose', Chiswell Green, Hertfordshire

Gunby Hall (NT), near Skegness, Lincolnshire

Hestercombe House, near Taunton, Somerset

Malmesbury Abbey Gardens, Malmesbury, Wiltshire

Myddelton House, Enfield, London

Nunnington Hall (NT), near Helmsley, North Yorkshire

Polesden Lacey (NT), near Dorking, Surrey

Powis Castle (NT), near Welshpool, Powys

Royal Horticultural Society Garden, Wisley, near Woking, Surrey

Sissinghurst Castle Garden (NT), near Cranbrook, Kent

Spetchley Park Garden, near Worcester, Worcestershire

Tintinhull House (NT), near Yeovil, Somerset

Twilight, off-season, in the iris garden at the National Trust's Nunnington Hall, North Yorkshire.

List of Suppliers

UNITED KINGDOM

Bloms Bulbs, Primrose Nurseries,
Melchbourne, Beds MK44 1ZZ
Tel. 01234 709099 Fax 01234 709799
www.blomsbulbs.com

Claire Austin Hardy Plants, The Stone
House, Cramp Pool, Shifnal, Shropshire
TF11 8PE
Tel. 01952 463700 Fax 01952 463111
www.claireaustin-hardyplants.co.uk

Croftway Nursery, Yapton Road, Barnham,
Bognor Regis, West Sussex PO22 0BQ
Tel. 01243 552121 Fax 01243 552125
www.croftway.co.uk

The Iris Garden, 47 Station Road, Barnet,
Herts EN5 1PR
Tel./Fax 020 8441 1300
www.theirisgarden.co.uk

Kelways Limited, Barrymore Farm,
Langport, Somerset TA10 9EZ
Tel. 01458 250521 Fax 01458 253351
www.kelways.co.uk

Seagate Irises, Long Sutton by-pass,
Long Sutton, Lincs PE12 9RX
Tel. 01406 365138 Fax 01406 365447
www.irises.co.uk

Woottens of Wenhaston, Blackheath,
Wenhaston, Halesworth, Suffolk IP19 9HD
Tel. 01502 478258 Fax 01502 478888
www.woottensplants.co.uk

UNITED STATES & CANADA

Aitken's Salmon Creek Garden,
608 NW 119th St, Vancouver, Washington
Tel. 360 573 4472 Fax 360 576 7012
www.flowerfantasy.net

Argyle Acres, 910 Pioneer Circle East,
Argyle, Texas 76226
Tel. 940 464 3680 Fax 866 320 4747
www.argyleacres.com

Cooley's Gardens, P.O. Box 126NT,
Silverton, Oregon 97381
Tel. 503 873 5463 Fax 503 873 5812
www.cooleysgardens.com

McMillen's Iris Garden, R.R.#1, Norwich,
Ontario N0J 1P0
Tel. 519 468 6508 Fax 519 468 3214
www.execulink.com~iris

Phoenix Flower Farm, 2620 Lamson Road,
Phoenix, New York 13135
Tel. 315 695 6777
www.phoenixflowerfarm.com

Schreiners Iris Gardens, 3625 Quinaby
Road NE, Salem, Oregon 97303
Tel. 800 525 2367
www.schreinersgardens.com

Sutton's Iris Gardens
16592 Road 208, Porterville, California
Tel. 559 784 5107 Fax 559 784 6701
www.suttoniris.com

Willow Bend Farm, 1154 Hwy 65, Eckert,
Colorado 81418
Tel. 970 835 3389
www.willowbendirisfarm.com

AUSTRALIA

Yarrabee Garden & Iris
C/- Post Office, One Tree Hill
SA 5114
Tel. 08 8280 7338
www.yarrabee.net

Iris Haven
P.O. Box 83, Pennant Hills
NSW 1715
Tel. 02 9144 3805 Fax 02 9440 0663
www.irishaven.com.au

FRANCE

Bourdillon Iris, Route de Gy, BP 2,
41230 Soings en Sologne
Tel. 02 54 98 71 06
Fax 02 54 98 76 76
www.bourdillon.com

Cayeux S.A., BP 35,
45501 Gien Cedex
Tel. 0800 096 4811
Fax 02 38 67 84 98
www.iris-cayeux.com

Iris Bertrand, Domaine de la Frégère,
Av. Mas de Faugère, 34150 Gignac
Tel./Fax 04 67 57 37 11
www.iris-bertrand.com

Iris en Provence, Chemin des Maures,
83400 Hyères
Tel. 04 94 65 98 30 Fax 04 94 35 24 91
www.iris-en-provence.com

Select Bibliography

IRIS SOCIETY WEBSITES

British Iris Society
www.britishirissociety.org.uk

American Iris Society
www.irises.org

Canadian Iris Society
www.members.rogers.com/cdn-iris

Historic Iris Preservation Society
www.worldiris.com

Italian Iris Society
www.irisfirenze.it

Société Française des Iris et Plantes Bulbeuses
www.iris-bulbeuses.org

The South Australian Iris Society
www.labdude.com/SAIris/index.htm

AUSTIN, Claire, *Irises: the Classic Bearded Varieties*, Quadrille (2001)

CAVE, N. L., *The Iris*, Faber & Faber (1959)

CAYEUX, Richard, *L'Iris, une fleur royale*, Éditions Mauryflor (1996)

DYKES, W. R., *The Genus Iris*, Cambridge University Press (1913), reprinted Dover Publications (1974)

DYKES, W.R., *A Handbook of Garden Irises*, Hopkinson (1924)

GROSVENOR, Graeme, *Iris: Flower of the Rainbow*, Simon & Schuster Int. (1999)

HAGER, Ben, *The Iris: the Rainbow Flower*, Thames & Hudson (1989)

LAWTON, Barbara Perry, *Magic of Irises*, Fulcrum (1998)

MATHEW, Brian, *The Iris*, Batsford (1981)

RANDALL, Harry, *Irises*, Batsford (1969)

STEBBINGS, Geoff, *The Gardener's Guide to Growing Irises*, David & Charles (1997)

Bulletins and yearbooks of the American Iris Society and British Iris Society.

Acknowledgements & Picture Credits

Many thanks to Barbara Mercer for her support throughout; to Mike Calnan, Bill Malecki, Fiona Screen and Margaret Willes for reviewing the text; to Julian and Wendy Browse at Seagate Irises, Michael Loftus at Woottens and David Root at Kelways; to National Trust head gardeners Christine Brain, Sarah Cook and Deborah Evans; Jim Marshall; Christine Murphy at Myddelton House; Margaret Criddle and Suz Winspear of the British Iris Society; Mike Lowe of the Historic Iris Preservation Society; Beth Chatto; Lady Rose Hare; the staff of the RHS Lindley Library.

Ashmolean Museum, Oxford: p.9; British Library, London: p.10; Julian Browse, Seagate Irises: p.64, p.70; Mark Fiennes: p.31, p.47, p.73, p.87; Mike Lowe, Historic Iris Preservation Society: p.20, p.45, p.63, p.85; Brenda Norrish: back cover, p.7, p.29, p.37, p.50, p.51, p.57, p.68, p.69, p.79, p.81, p.91; NTPL/Andrew Butler: p.93; NTPL/Neil Campbell-Sharp: p.21; NTPL/Eric Crichton: p.78; NTPL/Lee Frost: p.6; NTPL/John Hammond: p.12; NTPL/Geoff Morgan: p.14; NTPL/Stephen Robson: cover, p.19, p.32, p.33, p.34, p.43, p.49, p.59, p.61; NTPL/David Sellman: p.25; James Parry: p.22, p.84; Laurence Reed: p.1, p.2, p.26, p.27, p.35, p.38, p.39, p.41, p.66, p.67, p.71, p.82, p.83, p.88, p.89; David Root, Kelways Nursery: p.53, p.55, p.65.

NTPL: National Trust Photo Library